Get to Work
with
Science
and
Technology

Exploring Distant Worlds
as a
# Space Robot Engineer

by Ruth Owen

**Consultants:**

Kevin Yates
Fellow of the Royal Astronomical Society

Professor John Bridges
Planetary Scientist, University of Leicester, UK

Ruby Tuesday Books

Published in 2016 by Ruby Tuesday Books Ltd.

Editor: Mark J. Sachner
Designer: Emma Randall
Production: John Lingham

Photo Credits:
Alamy: Cover; Bridges, Professor John: 19 (top); NASA: 5 (top); NASA/
Bill Ingalls: 4, 18 (bottom); NASA/JPL: 6, 10, 16 (center), 19; NASA/JPL-
Caltech: 11 (top), 12, 13, 14, 15, 16 (left), 16 (right), 17, 20 (top), 22;
NASA/JPL-Caltech/MSSS: 11 (bottom), 20 (bottom), 21, 22–23, 23
(top); NASA/JPL-Caltech/MSSS/Jason Major: Cover, 5 (bottom); NASA/
JPL-Pioneer Aerospace: 9; NASA/Public Domain: Cover, 7, 8, 16 (top),
18 (top), 24, 25, 26, 27; Ruby Tuesday Books: 30; Shutterstock:
Cover, 2–3, 28–29.

Library of Congress Control Number:  2015907065

ISBN 978-1-910549-38-4

Printed and published in the United States of America

For further information including rights and permissions requests,
please contact our Customer Service Department at 877-337-8577.

# Contents

# We're Safe on Mars!

It's the evening of August 5, 2012. The place is **mission control** at **NASA**'s Jet Propulsion Laboratory (JPL) in California. **Engineers**, scientists, and controllers are watching computer screens and waiting. Millions of miles from Earth, the robot **rover** *Curiosity* is hurtling toward the surface of Mars.

The final minutes of the robot's journey to Mars slowly tick by. Then NASA engineer Al Chen makes the announcement everyone has been waiting for.

"Touchdown confirmed—we're safe on Mars!"

Mission control erupts. People cheer, clap, hug, and cry. Tonight is the end of a very long journey. But it's just the beginning of a robot's incredible mission on a distant world.

Engineers and scientists in mission control celebrate *Curiosity*'s safe arrival on Mars.

When *Curiosity* landed on Mars, the red planet was about 154 million miles (248 million km) from Earth.

It took more than 10 years and the hard work of thousands of people to send *Curiosity* to Mars.

A *Curiosity* selfie from Mars in 2015

*Curiosity*'s engineers thought of everything. They even designed equipment that lets the robot send selfies back to Earth!

# Building Space Robots

Mars is a hostile world. It's colder than the Arctic in winter, and the thin air is made up of poisonous gases. It's no place for human explorers and scientists. It's possible, however, for a robot like *Curiosity* to survive and work in this environment.

Today, robots are used to do work in space that is dangerous for humans to do. Designing and building these space robots is the job of an engineer.

Some space robot engineers are mechanical engineers. They design and build a robot's structure, or skeleton. Electrical engineers work on the electronics that power and control the robot.

Computer engineers design and build a robot's computer "brain." They also write the computer **software** that allows the robot to move, carry out tasks, and even think for itself.

In 1997, tiny *Sojourner* became the first rover to explore Mars. Here, engineers are preparing the robot for its mission.

Dextre

Dextre is a robot that makes repairs on the outside of the International Space Station (ISS). It does many jobs that astronauts once had to do. Having Dextre onboard means astronauts now make fewer dangerous spacewalks outside the ISS.

International Space Station (ISS)

# How to Design a Robot

How do space robot engineers decide what to build?

## Defining the Problem

Engineers design and build machines that provide a solution to a problem. The problem could be, how do we fix a space station without endangering its human crew? How can we explore a planet that has poisonous air? Or how can we bring samples back from Mars?

The answer to the problem is to build a robot.

## Researching

Engineers carry out research. What tasks does the robot need to do? How will it get into space? What is the **budget** for the project?

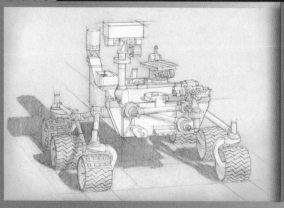
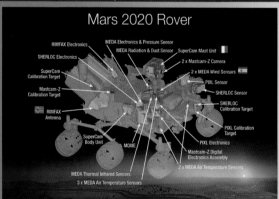

### Mars 2020 Rover

RIMFAX Electronics
SHERLOC Electronics
SuperCam Calibration Target
Mastcam-Z Calibration Target
RIMFAX Antenna
SuperCam Body Unit
MEDA Thermal Infrared Sensors
3 x MEDA Air Temperature Sensors
MOXIE
MEDA Electronics & Pressure Sensor
MEDA Radiation & Dust Sensor    SuperCam Mast Unit
2 x Mastcam-Z Camera
2 x MEDA Wind Sensors
PIXL Sensor
SHERLOC Sensor
SHERLOC Calibration Target
PIXL Calibration Target
PIXL Electronics
Mastcam-Z Digital Electronics Assembly
2 x MEDA Air Temperature Sensors

This sketch and 3D plan show design ideas for *Mars 2020*. This new robot rover is planned for launch to Mars in 2020.

## Designing

Next, engineers think up design ideas. When several people discuss ideas together, it's often called brainstorming. Once a design idea is chosen, engineers produce plans of the design. The plans might be drawn on paper or created using a computer program.

## Testing a Prototype

Next, engineers build a **prototype**, or test version, of the robot. The prototype is tested thoroughly and the test results are analyzed. Often parts of the design don't work, but this is not a bad thing. When a design fails, it allows an engineer to redesign and improve the robot idea.

Finally, the robot design is fully tested and it is ready to be built for real!

Space robot engineers work in offices and **laboratories**. In the office, they might design robots on a computer. In the lab, they build prototypes, carry out testing, and assemble the robots.

In order to land a robot rover on another planet, engineers also have to design, test, and build landing equipment. Here, engineers are testing *Curiosity*'s giant parachute.

# Designing a Mars Robot

In the late 1990s, a team of engineers and scientists at NASA began work on an exciting new project—the Mars Science Laboratory (MSL) mission. The mission would try to answer the question: *Does Mars have, or did it ever have, an environment that could support life?* *Curiosity* was the robot designed by the MSL team to go to Mars and carry out this mission.

| Curiosity | |
|---|---|
| Length: | 10 feet (3 m) |
| Width: | 9 feet (2.7 m) |
| Height: | 7 feet (2.1 m) |
| Weight: | 2,000 pounds (907 kg) |
| Length of arm: | 7 feet (2.1 m) |
| Top speed: | 100 feet (30 m) an hour |

Water is essential for life. So *Curiosity* would look for evidence that there was once water on Mars. It would also look for clues that Mars was once home to **microscopic** living things called **microbes**.

An artist created this illustration of *Curiosity* to show the world what the new robot would look like.

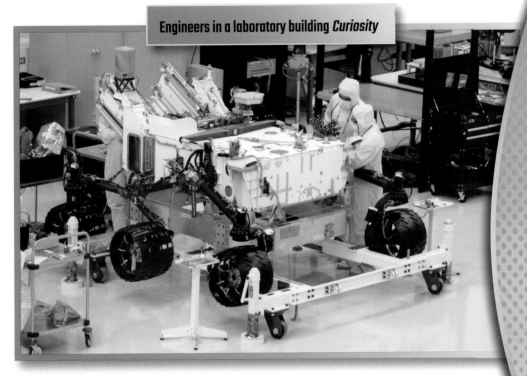

Engineers in a laboratory building *Curiosity*

*Curiosity* would be the largest robot to ever land on another world. Just like a mobile laboratory, it would be fitted with a range of scientific instruments. The robot would use the instruments to analyze rocks and soil on Mars. The team's design for *Curiosity* also included 17 cameras so the robot could photograph and film the planet's surface—and itself!

This photo was taken by *Curiosity*'s Mars Descent Imager (MARDI) camera. MARDI was designed to take photos as the robot descended toward the surface of Mars.

Engineers test *Curiosity*'s MARDI camera and adjust its focus.

# Test-Driving *Scarecrow*

At the same time that it was building *Curiosity*, the engineering team also built a lighter, stripped-back test version, or "stunt double." It is known as *Scarecrow*. *Scarecrow* weighed the same on Earth as *Curiosity* would weigh on Mars under the planet's lower **gravity**.

On Mars, *Curiosity* would need to drive up and down slopes. It would have to maneuver over soft sand, hard, compacted sand, and rocky ground. The engineering team had to be sure that *Curiosity* would not get stuck while traveling on Mars. This would be a catastrophe that could end the mission!

*Scarecrow* carried out test drives in the Mojave Desert in California. It was also tested at the Mars Yard. This area is a **simulation** of the surface of Mars built at NASA's Jet Propulsion Laboratory (JPL).

*Scarecrow* tries driving over a rock in the JPL Mars Yard.

*Scarecrow* doesn't have an onboard computer, or "brain." So it was playfully named after the Scarecrow, the character in *The Wizard of Oz* who lacks a brain. During test drives, the robot is connected by a cable to a computer operated by an engineer.

*Scarecrow* is still hard at work. It tests out maneuvers on Earth. Then driving instructions are uploaded to *Curiosity* on Mars.

Scarecrow

Engineer Amanda Steffy recreates Martian sand dunes in the Mojave Desert for a test drive.

# Clean Rooms and Bunny Suits

When *Curiosity* went to Mars, the mission team had to be sure the robot carried no microbes, or bacteria, from Earth. International space laws state that humans must not **contaminate** the planets, moons, or other space objects we explore.

Also, microbes from Earth could affect the results of an experiment on Mars. For example, microbes from Earth might get into a sample of Martian soil that *Curiosity* was testing. Then the scientists would have to figure out if the microbes were actually Martian or were in fact earthly hitchhikers!

Like all space robots or spacecraft, *Curiosity* was built in a clean room. This is a laboratory that's kept sterile, or free of bacteria. No contamination from the outside world is allowed to enter.

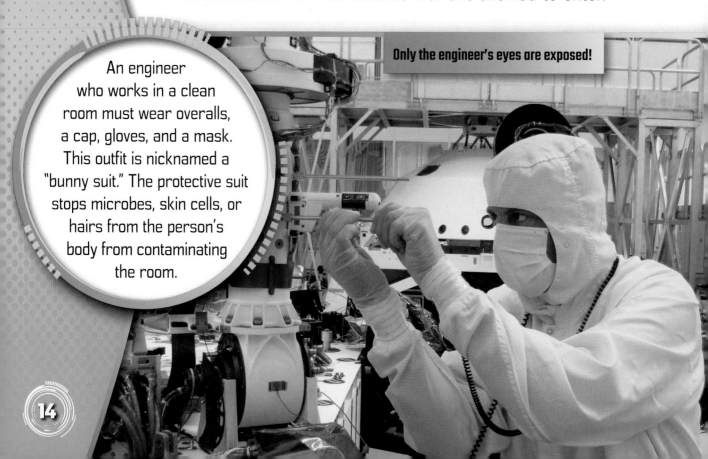

An engineer who works in a clean room must wear overalls, a cap, gloves, and a mask. This outfit is nicknamed a "bunny suit." The protective suit stops microbes, skin cells, or hairs from the person's body from contaminating the room.

Only the engineer's eyes are exposed!

Robot arm

A team of engineers in a clean room runs tests on *Curiosity*'s robot arm.

No one knows how bunny suits got their name. Possibly it comes from one-piece bunny costumes worn at Easter.

# The EDL Team

As *Curiosity* slowly came to life, another team of engineers was hard at work building the equipment to land the robot on Mars.

*Curiosity* is large and heavy, and it would be hurtling toward Mars at 13,000 miles per hour (20,900 km/h). The EDL (Entry, Descent, and Landing) team had a big challenge on their hands. To safely deliver the robot to the surface, they designed a giant parachute and a sky crane. As the EDL team waited in mission control that night in 2012, they watched their plans and ideas come to life.

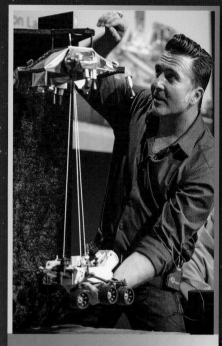

EDL engineer Adam Steltzner uses models to demonstrate the sky crane.

**Aeroshell**

*Curiosity* packed inside the aeroshell

**Heat shield**

*Curiosity* flew to Mars in a craft called an aeroshell.

With just seven minutes of its journey to go, the craft plunged into Mars's **atmosphere**. The aeroshell's heat shield protected the craft from the scorching heat.

Traveling through Mars's atmosphere slowed the craft. Then the aeroshell's giant parachute was deployed. As the aeroshell got closer to the ground, the heat shield detached and fell away.

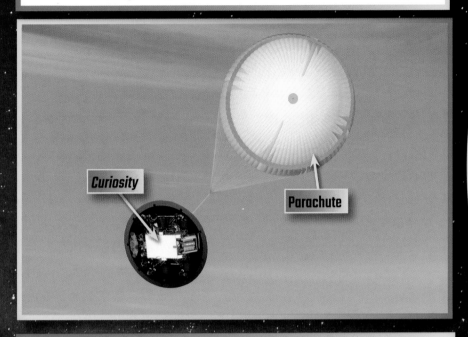

Curiosity

Parachute

The descent stage craft and *Curiosity* dropped from the aeroshell. Rocket boosters powered and controlled the craft's flight.

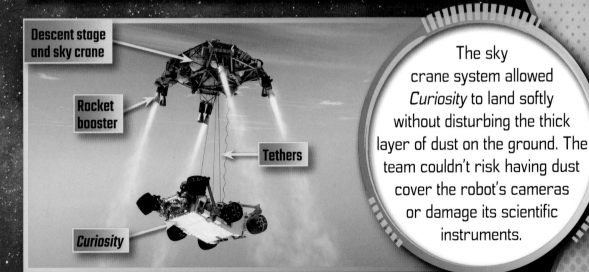

Descent stage and sky crane

Rocket booster

Tethers

Curiosity

The sky crane system allowed *Curiosity* to land softly without disturbing the thick layer of dust on the ground. The team couldn't risk having dust cover the robot's cameras or damage its scientific instruments.

Finally the sky crane system lowered *Curiosity* safely to the ground on tethers.

There were a million things that could have gone wrong. Thanks to the skill of the EDL team, nothing did!

# The Mission Scientists

Hundreds of scientists from around the world developed and planned *Curiosity*'s scientific mission. They gathered at JPL to witness the robot's landing. Once *Curiosity* was safely on Mars, the mission scientists worked as a team to carefully test the robot's instruments on Mars for the first time. Then, each day, they planned the robot's work and experiments.

Science is all about asking questions and doing research. As each new photo from *Curiosity* was downloaded, the mission scientists had lots of new questions and wanted to know more and more!

This is the first photo that *Curiosity* sent back to Earth. The mission's engineers and scientists were thrilled to see the robot's wheels safely on the planet's surface.

One of the mission scientists was Professor John Bridges from the United Kingdom. John was part of the ChemCam team. This device fires a laser beam that **vaporizes** rock. A special camera captures the flash as the rock is vaporized. Then light captured by the camera is analyzed to discover what chemicals the rock contains. Certain chemicals can help show if there was once life on Mars.

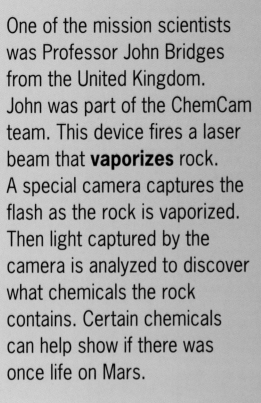
Prof. John Bridges, University of Leicester

This illustration shows *Curiosity* vaporizing rock with its laser beam.

# Driving a Robot Rover

As of July 2015, *Curiosity* is still hard at work on Mars. The team of engineers that controls the robot is known as the rover drivers.

Earth and Mars are many millions of miles apart. A signal from Earth can take 20 minutes to reach *Curiosity*. Therefore, it's not possible to give the robot commands and get an instant response. To safely control *Curiosity*, every second of its day is planned in advance.

NASA scientist Katie Stack Morgan studying images from *Curiosity*

*Curiosity*'s tire tracks

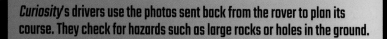

*Curiosity*'s drivers use the photos sent back from the rover to plan its course. They check for hazards such as large rocks or holes in the ground.

Each night, as the Sun sets on Mars, *Curiosity* takes a break. The team on Earth then works through the night. They plan every inch the robot will travel and every action it will take the next day. Then *Curiosity*'s "To Do" list for the day is uploaded to the robot.

Driving the rover isn't done with a joystick or console—just a keyboard. To give *Curiosity* its instructions, a rover driver keys in hundreds of commands in computer **code**.

*Curiosity*'s drivers command the robot to take photos of its tires and other parts. Engineers check these photos for damage to the rover.

# Martian Superstars

The teamwork between engineers, scientists, and a robot has made the Mars Science Laboratory (MSL) mission a great success. So far, *Curiosity* has made several important discoveries.

*Curiosity* discovered a dried-up streambed. This proved that billions of years ago, streams flowed on Mars. The robot drilled into rock and found tiny amounts of the chemicals carbon, oxygen, hydrogen, nitrogen, sulfur, and phosphorus. These chemicals show that some areas of Mars had environments that were friendly to life.

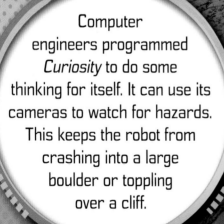

Computer engineers programmed *Curiosity* to do some thinking for itself. It can use its cameras to watch for hazards. This keeps the robot from crashing into a large boulder or toppling over a cliff.

*Curiosity*'s robotic arm undergoes tests in the lab.

*Curiosity*'s robotic arm using a drill on Mars. The engineers who built *Curiosity* get to see their work in action on another planet.

One day astronauts may travel to Mars. The amount of **radiation** on Mars is harmful to humans, though. So *Curiosity* has studied the levels of radiation on the planet. This research will be used to keep astronauts safe if they go to Mars.

A hole drilled by *Curiosity* in Mars rock

*Curiosity* takes photos of itself using a camera on its long arm. This image was pieced together from shots taken at different angles, so it was possible to leave out the arm.

# Robot Astronauts

The mission for *Curiosity*'s engineers was to send a robot scientist to Mars. The engineers developing a space robot called *Robonaut* had a very different challenge.

In space, astronauts often have to carry out tasks nicknamed the 3Ds—jobs that are dull, dangerous, or dirty. Could a robot astronaut be designed to do these jobs?

A robot could carry out dull and dirty tasks such as checking and fixing equipment. It could do dangerous work, such as making repairs to the outside of a space station. The robot would have to live and work alongside a human crew, though. It would also need to use the same switches, tools, and other equipment. The engineers' solution was to build a humanoid robot—*Robonaut*!

Engineers have built four *Robonauts*.

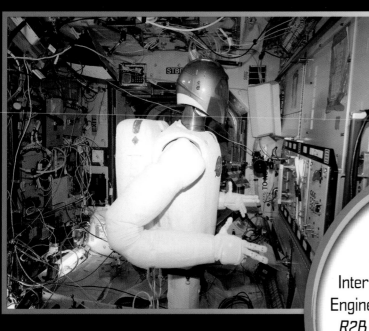

In 2011, *Robonaut 2B* became a crew member on the International Space Station (ISS). Engineers designed flexible legs for *R2B* with gripping feet called end effectors. The robot holds onto the space station with its feet. This leaves its hands free to do work.

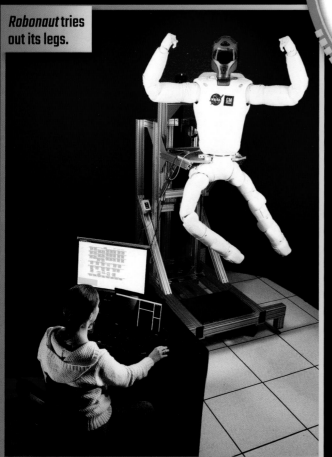

*Robonaut* tries out its legs.

*Robonaut*'s end effectors can grip rails and other parts of the ISS.

End effectors

# Creating *Robonaut*

To create *Robonaut*'s human-like hands, engineers studied the insides, or anatomy, of human hands and arms. They designed mechanical tendons to control the robot's hands. Tendons are the strong cords that attach human muscles to bones. *Robonaut*'s tendons allow its fingers to stiffen for extra force when it uses a tool such as a screwdriver. If *Robonaut* is handling a delicate science sample, the tendons can give the robot a softer grip.

*Robonaut*'s head contains cameras that act as the robot's eyes. Its computer brain is actually inside its chest.

*Robonaut*'s engineering team used computers to design the robot. Then, piece by piece, the robot came to life on workbenches in a laboratory.

An engineer runs tests on *Robonaut*'s software.

An engineer building *Robonaut*

*Robonaut*'s hands are fitted with sensors that allow it to feel what it's holding.

Robonaut gets fitted with its flight suit.

An astronaut wearing virtual reality equipment controls Robonaut.

Robonaut can be controlled by a person wearing a virtual reality mask and gloves. The robot makes the same movements as the controller. The robot can also be controlled by commands keyed into a computer.

Robonaut

# Space Robots of the Future

What kinds of space robots will the engineers of the future create?

NASA engineers are currently working on plans for *Mars 2020*. This new robot rover will look similar to *Curiosity*. Its main science goals are to search for signs of past life, collect rock samples for possible return to Earth, and test technologies for future human missions.

Engineers are working with doctors on a plan to train *Robonaut* to be a doctor. One day, robot doctors might take care of crews on spacecraft or space stations.

To design and build a space robot, engineers and scientists use technology, science, math, and computer skills. Being an engineer is all about having big ideas—and then bringing them to life!

The engineers that built *Curiosity* didn't get to go to Mars. They did, however, write letters that were put onto microchips and carried into space by their robot.

# Get to Work as a Space Robot Engineer

## What subjects should I study to be a robot engineer?
You will need to study and enjoy science subjects and math. At a college or university, you will study engineering, physics, and computer science.

## How soon can I get started?
Building robots can be a great hobby, so find out if there's a robotics club at your school or go online to check out opportunities near your home.

## Where do robotics engineers work?
If you want to build space robots, you might get to work with a space agency such as NASA, CSA (Canadian Space Agency), or ESA (European Space Agency). Some robotics engineers work for companies that produce other types of robots. They build robots that fight fires, explore under the ocean, or work in factories.

## When does a space robot engineer work?
If an engineer is working on a space exploration project, it can mean working 12 or 14 hours a day. If a launch date is approaching, it cannot be missed. So engineers may work weekends and through holidays—whatever it takes to hit the mission deadline!

### Design a Robot Rover

NASA is working on robot explorers called *K10* robots. These robots could be sent to other planets or the Moon. The robots would explore and send information back to Earth. The information will help scientists plan missions for human astronauts.

In this activity, you will create a design for a robot rover and build a prototype from recycled materials.

**Materials:**
- A notebook and pen
- Graph paper
- Colored pencils or pens
- Scissors
- Glue and tape
- Recycled materials from around the home, such as cardboard, plastic bottles, bottle tops, old DVDs, silver paper, drinking straws, string

**Procedure:**

1. Begin by thinking about these questions and doing research.

   *Where is your robot rover headed, and what tasks will it do?*

   *How will it land on a moon, planet, or other space object?*

   *What problems must your design solve?*

2. Think about design ideas. Once you've chosen an idea to develop, make a sketch or plan of your design on graph paper. Label all the parts of your design and name your rover.

3. Create a list of materials needed to build your prototype.

4. Gather your materials and start building your prototype.

5. As you build, keep notes about what's working and what's not. Make improvements to your rover design.

6. When your prototype is finished, evaluate your rover. How does it compare to your original drawing? Does your design solve the problems you identified in step 1?

7. Write a short statement to convince NASA that they should build your robot design.

# Glossary

**atmosphere** (AT-muh-sfeer)
A layer of gases around a planet, moon, or star.

**budget** (BUHD-jit)
The amount of money to be spent on a particular project.

**code** (KODE)
A language of letters, numbers, and symbols used to give instructions to a computer. A rover's driver uses computer code to give commands to the rover.

**contaminate** (kuhn-TAM-uh-nate)
To harm or make something unclean by introducing something dirty or dangerous.

**engineer** (en-juh-NIHR)
A person who uses math, science, and technology to design and build machines.

**gravity** (GRA-vuh-tee)
The force that causes objects to be pulled toward other objects.

**laboratory** (LA-bruh-tor-ee)
A room or building where there is equipment that can be used to carry out experiments and other scientific studies.

**microbes** (MY-krobes)
Living things that are so tiny they can only be seen with a microscope, not with a person's eyes alone. The bacteria, or germs, that cause disease are types of microbes.

**microscopic** (mye-kroh-SKOP-ik)
Only visible when viewed through a microscope.

**mission control**
(MISH-uhn kuhn-TROHL)
A command center on Earth from which people control a space mission.

**NASA** (NAS-ah)
A group of scientists and space experts in the United States. NASA studies space and builds spacecraft. The letters in NASA stand for "National Aeronautics and Space Administration."

**prototype** (PROH-tuh-tipe)
The first version, or test version, of something, such as a vehicle or machine. The final version is developed from the prototype.

**radiation** (ray-dee-AY-shun)
A type of invisible energy that travels through space. High levels of radiation can be harmful to living things.

**rover** (ROH-vur)
A robot with wheels that is used to explore a moon, planet, or other space object.

**simulation** (sim-yoo-LAY-shuhn)
A pretend version of something, such as a place.

**software** (SAWFT-ware)
The programs that are used to operate computers.

**vaporize** (VAY-pur-ize)
To turn something into vapor, or gas.

# Index

# Read More

**Forest, Christopher**. *Robot Competitions (Edge Books)*. Mankato, MN: Capstone Press (2013).

**Owen, Ruth**. *Robots in Space (It's a Fact!)*. New York: Ruby Tuesday Books (2015).

# Learn More Online

To learn more about space robot engineers, go to:
**www.rubytuesdaybooks.com/spacerobotengineers**